Notes on Shapeshifting

poems and other stories

by gabi abrão

Not a Cult
Los Angeles, CA

For information, contact books@notacult.media.

ISBN: 978-1-945649-82-0

Edited by Rhiannon McGavin
Proofread by Charlotte Renner
Cover Design by Shaun Roberts

Not a Cult
Los Angeles, CA
Printed in Canada

CHAPTERS

every few hours
i swear i'm too alive
and i wouldn't trade it for
Anything

a rushing waterfall
is a master of stillness

ROMANCE IS A MEDIUM AND A KISS IS A PORTAL

"Everything in the world began
with a yes. One molecule said yes
to another molecule and life was born."

— Clarice Lispector, *The Hour of the Star*

This is Why Sharing a Joint and a Bottle of Wine in a Parking Lot With You Felt Better Than Five Courses on the Rooftop of That Famous Hotel

I often question if the quest for pleasure and romance in life is a direct influence of excess-driven, stimulation-starved, consumerist constructs. But it isn't at all. It's the only humanity we have - our lust and life force at its simplest forms and manifestations. It makes the world spin and yet we keep attempting to dilute the message, only allowing the occasional artist to remind us who we are.

When I think of pleasure and romance, I do not think of skyscraper penthouses and seafood towers and first-class leg room. I think of being naked in the sunshine on a cotton towel near a stream, then being fucked in that stream, laughing while I take my post-penetration pee. I think of giggling where there ought not to be giggling, I think of indulgence - the type of indulgence that challenges your emotions, not your bank account.

As a culture, I believe we need to fight to remember these pleasures and the simplicity of their source. The consumerist format gives us multiple tangible vessels and systems to play pretend with this inner call for indulgence, this pursuit of pleasure - to gamble, to set the scene - and yet, it is only just a tangible simulation that points at it, but never satiates it. A giant machine desperately trying to simulate a heart beat, and yet the heart itself prevails, unaware of the chaos it has caused by being misinterpreted. A soul's desire for indulgence is based in energy and feeling. It travels beyond any room, any structure, any purchase. The ego encounters this enticing sensation and proceeds to create a room anyway - only to hunt for itself again, within it.

don't kiss someone unless   you're dying to do so

Sometimes You Have to Ditch School
and Observe the Rituals of Creek Newts

Tatiana and I used to stash cargo pants and last season's worn out sneakers in our lockers for the many days that we chose to escape the routine noise of high school to be naked in the afternoon sun. Our school was located in the Pacific Palisades, minutes away from both the ocean and a mountain trail. To spend hours in fluorescent lit rooms with barred windows in such a landscape felt like a scam.

On the days where we truly couldn't shake this blatant sense of betrayal, we'd slip past the security guard, walk along the chain-link fence toward Temescal Canyon Park, then hike past the waterfall into the creek beyond it, stripping off all of our clothes. We'd find a smooth rock in the sunshine to take our backs, our eternal goal being an even, unending tan across our skin - a premature offering to the boys we dreamt of one day sharing our nudity with. In spring, past the bridge and that waterfall, it was just us and the newts.

A strange incident surfaced as we observed these animals - the newts began to crowd their bodies together into tight, unified, spherical forms and roll down the creek. Solo newts swam from all directions to attach themselves to the nearest blob like sticky magnets. This continued all afternoon. I have a vivid memory of these vibrant balls of newts tussling through the water below our naked, young bodies -

everyone's flesh sparkling. We had never seen anything like it. An intentioned, absurd mystery that only nature can produce.

I would google information about newts months later, only to find that these amorphous forms we witnessed were actually orgies, as their mating practice entails multiple males taking turns penetrating a single female. It comes as no surprise that the portal of sex, the portal of birth, was placed at the center of this passionate, animal phenomenon as well as this rebellious teenage ritual - the reason for this fleshy planet, the reason for everything.

I Am Allergic To Mosquitos and Your House is Full of Them

you text me a blurry photo
of a humongous dead boar in the bed of your truck
It is only your second day hunting and you do that
You tell me how you prayed before during and after,
you tell me how you're sharing the meat with the whole town
and you can't wait to make me tacos,
you say something about being primal

I moved here to write poetry and follow Twitter drama
tan here and there
Do everything I was doing in the city,
with a twist,
but two months in I fall for a man
who kills a giant boar on his second try
and has no feeling in his feet.
Who has a water tank on his roof
and a shower that is heated by the sun

When my landlord offered me a one year lease,
I negotiated down to 9 months
"like a pregnancy term" I said

The only primal part of me is that I love to fantasize
about getting impregnated during sex
even though I am on birth control.
And I love to pee outside,
like it is my territory.

I came here to wear gold earrings and swimsuits
but I am allergic to mosquitoes
and your house is full of them.

i serpent all over you, my heaven, my love. You hold
my melting face.

Yes I Miss You,

and I know you'd argue
the idea of you, the illusion of you,
the whole trick -

as if there always has to be one.

But I've gone
through the best of it
and the worst of it
I've applied both pressure
and distance
I've checked for truth
at every new hour
Lead search parties
town meetings
filled journals

and yet here I remain
stuck on the idea of you, the illusion of you,
the whole trick -

and I don't even have that.

Dumped

I'm slowly killing
the part of me
that is waiting

for stones to hit my windowpane
for flowers to grace my doorstep
for sixty calls to light up my screen

a new crush enters like an angel

Romance is a Medium
and a Kiss is a Portal

All acts of seduction and attraction are a practice in understanding the invisible. Everything in life is a medium. These mediums feed into one another, exposing the design of it all - a shared energy presenting a different face, different decoration. To develop a crush is to experience the power of your imagination, your will, it is to show us that when narrative and invisible force come together and point at a target, the body follows. To flirt with a lover is a practice in seducing your dreams. To witness the grand, shared life created in a relationship, only to witness its tragic end, is a practice in accepting death.

HOW TO HEAL HEARTBREAK

"The moon winks.
I'm a simp I think.
But I'm wrong.
I know what I am."

— Sandra Cisneros, *My Wicked Wicked Ways*

I wake up alone and I
mix the arugula and the spinach and the apples alone
And strands of hair split my face into sections
alone
And I wonder when to wash my sheets and my pillow cases
and my towels , alone   And I consider the future
        alone ,
and I worry about if I brush my teeth well enough , alone
And I light the candles and feel 20% holier now
                alone

I continue existing with the knowledge
that love dies like the power goes out

I Took Over Five Grams of Shrooms to Get Over My Soulmate but Then I Didn't Think of Him Once

Committed to a large amount, awaiting a death of sorts, awaiting a pain, a pang, a slap in the face. We built a fire that turned into more of a smoke signal. It burdened us all, but from it, we worked together with water to put it out - passing water through windows. Giggling, snickering. Feeling like creatures in a treehouse.

I collapse into the tiny carpeted stairs of the camper and laugh about how I literally don't care, for any of it, all of it, in the most beautiful way. "I just don't care," she says, hands up, laughing. In this dark blue flannel coat and brand new beige Timberlands. I just don't care. I marvel at the simple concept of doing. I say to myself - "I came here... to the woods to hang out with...friends, and I'm in an outfit, and...," I laugh and laugh. Wet eyes. A word remains on the tip of my tongue, and I never access it. It feels like barbie dolls, like the way the letter "F" sounds in the word "funny" or "wife." Focusing on such specific nothingness feels as honest as focusing on the somethings which are just as nothing, just as obsessive, the same circle.

My present mind only knows pleasure. My present mind believes humans are geniuses, over and over, as I'm surrounded by all of these inventions - the kettle, the heater, the computer. "Geniuses," I keep saying. And I'm almost angry, because in some ways I know I'm not supposed to feel that way, but I feel it. I want to scream it. We are all geniuses.

We peel tangerines, we burn the peels in the candles we lit at sunrise. Textures, new smells, a crinkling motion. And oh, how the tarot cards came to life then! The ocean, a real ocean on this tarot card. Moving, singing. Unbelievable. In our hands.

We see 3:33 on the microwave, bright green, digital, and the universe giggles and shakes along with us. The kitchen is a dollhouse kitchen, the wood grain dancing. I watch my favorite scene in *Endless Poetry*, a scene in the middle of the film with the puppets saying goodbye, their ceramic hands caressing one another. Everyone understands its beauty, laying around the compartment-like living room of the camper. Slumped, squishy bodies across pillows with smiles. We watch the pet snake drink water. Alluring thing, taking its time. "He never comes out for this long" - she says. "He knows" - we all say.

There are four of us. We're entertained by laser pointers, condensation passing through mugs, warmth, the moment itself. My hands are large, soft. The trees dance for us of course. They dance so much, too much. Radiant beings. The joy of connection. The magic of living, of observing. A vastness that extends beyond any betrayal.

I took over five grams of shrooms to get over a past lover, but then I didn't think of him once.

HOW TO HEAL HEARTBREAK

The guide below was written after the sudden close of a lengthy relationship with a perceived soulmate. It was during that stretch following a fresh loss that feels like pure survival. Bent on healing, I observed my reactions and habits to build an emotional map. This emotional map is as follows:

STEP 1. DECIDE TO HEAL
Often, attaching to the situation and continuing to identify with the person is a way of keeping them alive in your heart. We'd rather be tortured and remain obsessed over a past relationship than move on. Having them in our lives as an enemy feels better than not at all. Make the choice.

STEP 2. BE PHYSICALLY PREPARED
Have plenty of water by your bed for when you wake up, don't go too long without eating, shower daily or more - prioritize maintenance. When your mood is lower than usual, every bit counts. A slight dehydration can make a sad morning into a devastating one. A missed meal can turn a temporary hiccup into a tantrum. Furthermore, your immune system gets depleted when you're that sad. Be prepared for possible colds and flare-ups, and know that it's just a pesky result of your passing pain being felt by your body.

STEP 3. CRYING

You will want to cry a lot of the time, and you may surprise yourself with how often, and in what moments, the urge arrives. Let it happen, and hold no shame for this cleansing process. Crying reduces stress hormones and can often serve as a portal to a new feeling. The flood will stop sooner than you think.

STEP 4. DREAMS

You will dream about your ex significantly following the break-up. Be prepared for this. The dreams will vary from sweet and healing to downright evil and day-ruining. Remember that your ex's image in your dreams is serving as a placeholder in your subconscious for complex feelings and questions.

These dreams are not insights or truths on the situation, as they're being formed by your perception alone - your wounded perception that you can't truly trust right now. If you wake up from an ex dream, dismiss it immediately. Do not search for prophecies or truths. Dwelling on a dream and its hidden meanings, especially in the early stages where nothing makes sense, will ruin your morning and send you down ungrounded spirals.

STEP 5. WHEN EMOTIONS GET BIG, DON'T MAKE ANY SUDDEN MOVEMENTS

Some days, you'll wake up full of rage and think you know exactly what to say. Your whole body will reach for your phone to produce the truth-telling paragraph text of a lifetime. Pause, drink water, have your breakfast. Type these urges into a word document instead of a message. If it's the right thing to do, your words will still sound succinct after a few hours - or better yet, days - have passed. If it isn't, it'll sound like a jumble of misdirected reactivity and make you cringe. When emotions get large and induce affirmative action, take your time with the actions.

STEP 6. MANAGE DIGITAL ILLUSIONS
Don't hesitate to mute or block your ex - and even their friends - on social media if you have to. Social media is already an illusion that induces flawed perception, insecurities around self-image and status, and incomplete storytelling that pushes us to fill in the blanks. This factor plus heartbreak is a chaotic, useless mix. You are not missing anything.

STEP 7. DO NOT IDENTIFY EVERY LOW EMOTION WITH THE HEARTBREAK
When you're heartbroken, every low point or bad mood is immediately attested to the heartbreak. It becomes the perpetrator of every hint of misfortune or sadness that enters your life. Although this will be true every once in a while, it isn't always. Remember how, even when you were in the greatest points of the relationship, you still had off days and depressive episodes? Yeah. Don't give the heartbreak all the credit and power, as it is not the keeper of every emotion. Let your sadness continue to exist for a multitude of reasons, or no reason at all.

STEP 8. RECALL THE INCOMPATIBILITIES

Post-heartbreak logic creates a grand tale of loss and defeat. It'll convince you that you lost your one and only, that your soulmate was snatched from your hands - all while completely glossing over the negatives. Take many moments to pause and remember the patterns that spoke of disharmony. Ground yourself in the facts of the situation that may not be flattering, including the clear fact that you are no longer together. Recall the disagreements and discomforts, recall the times you felt alone or misunderstood - anything that was lacking which you can now nourish elsewhere. Keeping yourself in check with your post-breakup storytelling, especially in your own mind, will keep you safe from illusory, stunting narratives.

STEP 9. TALK TO PEOPLE ABOUT IT, THEN DON'T

After my most devastating break-up, I found a lot of value in telling my boss, coworkers, friends, and family about what I was going through. I wasn't expecting this to be a point of healing, as the primary reason I had to share what happened with others was because I couldn't conceal how depressed and angry I was and had to offer an explanation. When you leave your work shift to cry in the bathroom for the third time that day, or you don't touch your favorite dish at the family dinner, there is no hiding.

To my surprise, it was deeply humanizing and helpful to discover how people reacted to my confession of heartbreak. What felt like an apology was met with words of affirmation. So many could relate to and understand the feeling, especially much older adults, who were full of support and personal stories. I now feel closer to all these people that I shared my pain with, and felt so seen during the process. By being honest with everyone, I could be more honest with myself. Most people have been heartbroken before, and most people love to talk about it, aware of the irrational power it holds. The felt connection is phenomenal. However, and this is important: Once you share your woes, don't make your heartbreak the main talking point in all your conversations. It is not your new identity. Talking about the situation on repeat is the same as circling over it in your head - it'll keep you there.

STEP 10. ACTIVELY CHANGE YOUR THOUGHTS

Settle on three positive visualizations, words, or scenarios that you can replace negative thoughts with on contact. Write them down. The minute that your imagination starts wandering into painful why's and how's, maneuver your psyche to replace them with these alternate thoughts. Think of the love you have for your pets, recite a simple self-empowering mantra, or reminisce on great memories with a best friend. For expert level, replace these negative thoughts with visions of your dream house piece by piece, down to the furniture choices and parties you wish to have, as a sort of manifestation exercise. Our mind is always in a thought loop, running through old memories and needless questions on autopilot, causing turmoil for no good reason. Actively feeding it another thought is not only possible, but greatly beneficial. This may be difficult at first, as with any mindfulness practice, because you are shifting an unconscious habit. But with effort and commitment, shifting the movies that play in your mind's eye will be second nature.

STEP 11. RECONNECT WITH YOUR BODY

When you get used to sharing your body with someone, it's a strange sensation to witness the empty space where touch once was. The process of connecting to your physical body and senses in solitude feels foreign and must be reintroduced. Reconnecting to your body will look different for everyone - some will take up a new workout routine, some will masturbate frequently, some will lounge in their favorite underwear, catching looks at themselves in the mirror. Whatever it is, take part in the reconnection process and make peace with the ghostly nature of it. Massage your own feet, take showers that are rich with scrubbing and touching, stretch often, wear clothing that feels great on your skin. Give yourself many moments of physical affection.

STEP 12. HANG OUT WITH YOUR REAL FRIENDS

Let your friends know emotionally where you're at every time you hang out, and do simple, time-passing activities. Watch silly reality shows or comedy specials, go to your favorite cafe with laptops doing work and sipping various beverages in silence, spend hours at the bookstore. Or, just exist together doing your own thing in the same room. Having easy, trusted company does wonders. Surround yourself with people who you don't feel pressure to entertain, who you can be comfortable with sharing a cry or a silence.

STEP 13. NARRATE YOURSELF AS IF IN A MOVIE

You are the protagonist in a passionate tale of overcoming oppressive pain in a journey toward resilience, self-love, and newfound independence. Write indulgent poetry, listen to redemption songs by lonesome cowboys, dress up in an outfit that makes you feel strong, take up a new hobby you can excel at, build yourself up. Enjoy performing the act of emotional conquest until it becomes your reality. All of that potent art about overcoming heartbreak exists for a reason, and now it's all for you.

STEP 14. LEAVE TOWN IF YOU CAN

Be a stranger in another city or take to nature. Wherever you go, make it an intentionally self-soothing trip. Turn off your phone if you can, bring a real camera and journal along with you, eat well, and truly explore the new terrain. Even if you're sad the entire time.

STEP 15. ACCEPT THAT IT'S OVER

It's over. They are not going to call you with regrets tomorrow, or next month. It's done, and they are not in your life. Even if they do try to come back, it will serve you to not expect it in the slightest. Hope and bargaining will keep you in the sludge and illusions for far too long, entertaining stories and scenarios that may never be. Do not indulge a situation that does not exist.

STEP 16. ACCEPT YOUR SHAME AND EMBARRASSMENT

Accept that you feel unwanted and unseen. Accept that you put work into something that didn't last, or result how you envisioned. Accept that you are feeling misunderstood and rejected. Accept that people are probably talking about you. Accept that your pain isn't linear or over. Do it kindly, with unconditional love. Our culture treats relationships as ventures with a clear "win" or "lose" - "win" being marriage or "forever" - and because of this inaccurate cultural narrative, break-ups naturally make us feel like complete losers. But relationships, and what they bring into our lives, are far more dimensional than that, regardless of where they lead. A break-up is not a failure. It is a re-route and an invitation to a new season of your life.

STEP 17. REMEMBER
You're stronger than you feel, and time passes quicker than you can imagine. One day, this event will just be a small set of poems in your journal, or a set of photos that do nothing other than make you laugh at what you were wearing at the time. Everyone has been deeply hurt or disrespected by another person at least once in their lives, and you are not alone. You will wake up and recognize yourself again, and it will be grand, it will be bigger than anything.

TIME IS NOT LINEAR AND LOVE NEVER LEAVES US

"You live in the image you have of the world. Every one of us lives in a different world, with different space and different time."

— Alejandro Jodorowsky

RIP Every Moment Before This One...

you know what i mean?

(but energy is eternal)
(so there are no deaths)
(only new lives)
(which is just as petty)

Venus Retrograde

When, once again,
narrative proves it does not exist.
The rules we made up
the lines we drew in the dirt
the non-negotiable statements;
(an ending!)
thrown out the top floor window
in a single motion
and all you can do is laugh
and laugh, and laugh
and begin again
(but there is no such thing as a beginning)

Time is Not Linear and Love Never Leaves Us

When I tell you
that I love being in love
there is no man in my life
There is no significant
other
that holds my gaze

When I tell you
that I love being in love,
it hits me when I'm alone
by a breezy window
It's summer and it's
the only window
in this house
that makes the heat beautiful

And when i tell you
that I love being in love -
I am light and moving
I am held and whole

all you can see is one of me
but there
are maybe six of me
Invisible
with caressing hands

When I tell you
That I love being in love
there is no end
to the sensation

No permission
that must be granted
When i tell you
that I love being in love
I mean it

Moment of Clarity No. 1:
Everything is Visiting

I am alone, dipping a brownie into coffee, blasting strong female voices out of a bluetooth speaker over the cold countertops in the kitchen of an empty, shared house. I am being visited by a wave of eternal clarity.

Right now, I am recalling the days that are lush with ideas and influence and seem to last forever... but also the days where I just give up and go right to sleep because I swear that the day has absolutely nothing for me. Both are heaven. Every moment is full of so many blatant symbols. How can life ever feel like anything other than poetry on a loop? A carousel of animals and mirrors as you build your own personal lexicon?

If you're in this euphoric headspace today, I celebrate with you. If you are not, I am here to remind you that this dimension exists, it will visit you again, and again, and sometimes it stays for one hour at breakfast, but sometimes it sticks around for a day, maybe three. And you'll feel it in the shower, and you'll feel it as you sip the second tea of the two in a day, and you'll feel it as you text your best friend who moved many miles away but is such a divine piece of your identity that physical distance doesn't alter a damn thing.

I am moved by everything and everyone that stayed a while, even if they departed. Today, I fall to my knees in appreciation for each and every single visit.

On Reveling In Time:
Birthday Ritual

Last year, I began a birthday ritual where I booked two nights at a hotel. One day and one night is spent alone, mapping and listening to the hotel, scheming and plotting; acquainting. I give myself a series of tasks - a to-do list, a syllabus - where events such as taking a bubble bath or observing the lobby paintings are taken seriously. I bring my favorite poetry books and revisit playlists of intensity's past. I manipulate time to move slower.

When you're alone, people reach out and talk to you more, too, and often surprises and experiences come through this. I once situated myself alone on the Petit Ermitage rooftop with hotel stationary at 2am, only to be immediately invited into a group of travelers whose unifying factor was their love for Burning Man and selling weed in copious, wholesale amounts. The older Italian man in the group, dawning a wide-brimmed hat and long gray beard, explained how he befriended a pack of wolves near his home by biting them on the nose. He then gave me advice on Los Angeles, growing older, and navigating the uncomfortable self-interest required in existing and creating. His words filled the thirty year gap between our experiences, and speaking to an eccentric elder felt like a classic coming-of-age event. Especially on a birthday, on a rooftop, in the middle of my twenties, in the middle of the night.

On day two, I invite friends and do the cake and the dinner and the celebration, and take advantage of all the information I gathered on day one. Hotels are such compact micro-worlds with a life of their own - they function like a body, and thrive on trust. Everything has a rhyme or reason in the hotel, but there is always some wiggle room for surprises and secrets within the structure itself or its visitors. Those who operate the space often indulge in this lore as well, and in the proper mood, collaborations are imminent. The shared context of leisure and transience unifies all participants in the grand body that is the hotel. It is a static location in constant movement, as all things are. In short, a design is shared, and anything is possible.

In terms of splitting the birthday into two - what is a birthday but a moment of half wallowing, half hyper-social celebrating? This ritual honors that fact, covering all bases into balance.

This year, twenty-twenty-one, I stayed at the Chateau Marmont. I had a ghostly day to myself, then threw a small, last-minute party in room 59. This historic Hollywood building in particular is highly significant to a pipe dream of my teenage self, who coveted the property and its mysteries. Reveling within its walls on my own terms felt dense and full.

I have this tale of my two best friends and I at fifteen years old, dressing up in thrifted dresses and heels and heading to Sunset Boulevard by way of the metro bus, in hopes of seeing the Chateau Marmont in the flesh. At the time, we were all obsessed with the following: Uptown Girls (2003), Courtney Love's band Hole, The Velvet Underground, Lana Del Rey, and thrifted negligees... the Chateau being a dominant, sought after character in that whole old-Hollywood, damsel in distress expression. Sunset Boulevard ended up being unsafe and chaotic and the Chateau was nowhere to be found. Cars were honking at us and our quest was a failure. We would later find out that the elusive castle was tucked up a driveway and certainly not the type of place that three misguided, wannabe-adult teenagers could show up to.

That night, we ended up stranded at a fluorescent-lit El Pollo Loco in a strip mall, where I got my period in the bathroom. One of our dads eventually picked us up. Feeling like a character in a video game that fails a level and is rapidly transported back to the mouth of it, we sat in his gray sedan, silent and guilty. I would go on to bury this memory until I was on the opposite end of it - recalling it twelve years later, on the balcony of room 59 in my underwear.

WORD GETS OUT
AND ALL OF A SUDDEN
    YOU'RE AT THE
            PETIT ERMITAGE

DRINKING WATER OUT OF
            A WINE GLASS)

I WISH I COULD TAKE
    THIS CARPETTED FLOOR
        HOME WITH ME

AND START OVER
    (BUT BEGIN FROM
        THIS POINT)

IS THAT NOT WHAT
    IS HAPPENING?

(I CAN'T TELL)

NOTES ON CHATEAU MARMONT
ROOM NO. 58

1. EVERY LIGHT / LAMP TURNS ON VERY
   DIFFERENTLY. SOMETIMES YOU WONDER HOW
   FOR A WHILE. IT ISN'T CLEAR AT FIRST.
   MAKES EACH ONE FEEL LIKE A CREATURE
   YOU ARE MAKING A MEMORY WITH.

2. MY ROOM FACES A BIG HILL FULL
   OF HOUSES. I AM ONE WINDOW FACING
   HUNDREDS OF WINDOWS. I WISH I HAD BINOCULARS.

3. "DIDN'T I" BY DARONDO IS ON THE
   ROOM'S BUILT-IN PLAYLIST. "FADE INTO YOU"
   MY MAZZY STAR IS ALSO.

4. YOU CAN RUN IN A CIRCLE IF
   YOU'D LIKE - THROUGH THE KITCHEN. GOOD
   FOR PACING ON THE PHONE OR
   DANCING ALONE.

5. THERE IS DENSE BAMBOO OUT BACK BY
   THE LONG STAIRCASE BY #3 & #4.

6. THE CARPET DOCUMENTS ALL OF YOUR
   FOOT STEPS.

7. BATH TUB FAUCET IS BEAUTIFUL, GREAT WATER
   FLOW. MAYBE THE BEST I'VE
   EVER SEEN.

8. THE BEST THING I CAN EVER DO FOR MYSELF IS TAKE MY TIME.

ETHER BODY

"What is real is not the external form,
but the essence of things...it is impossible
for anyone to express anything essentially
real by imitating its exterior surface."

— Constantin Brancusi

It is in Your Best Interest to Remain Aware of the Deep Vastness and Absurdity That is Your Existence

Anchoring yourself to the only proven truth - that life is a boundless mystery full of change and surprise and stimulation, you will feel less cheated by the nature of existence because you are living in pure awareness of it.

Clinging to narrative is wonderful until it shatters every single time - and why are we surprised every time? The only stable, eternal truth is the absurdity, the non-linearity, the inconsistency. The hero and the villain, the winner and the loser, the beginning, middle, end - it's all made up. A story for the sake of story-telling. An illusion of scale and order in a land where there is no definitive. It eases the mind temporarily - clapping at the end of the movie, pointing at the victor, reconstructing your memories into tales of reason and redemption. But what is the eternal town square? What is experience always guiding us back to?

There are few existential facts, some of which are: All of life is ephemeral and you will die; change is inevitable and constant; there is no certainty, only possible clues; what is unknown dominates the known.

And yet we spend the majority of our lives dwelling on the past, fearing death, suffering through change, and cursing at the world for its lack of answers. To live like this is to drive in the oncoming lane, dumbfounded as to why you are dodging traffic. It is to pet a dog in the opposite direction of its fur, wondering why you are meeting resistance. It is to push ceaselessly on a door that pulls open.

When your map fades into indistinguishable silhouettes; when the only sense you can muster is that of sight, smell, touch, taste, and sound; when life shoves you in the chest and offers a stark reminder that it has promised you absolutely nothing; Say to yourself - Ah yes, I recognize her.

This Vessel Holds Both the Observer and the Performer

The observer is of consciousness - the observer feels the truth of the world and the human condition and just feels blessed to witness this complex dimension.

The observer is eternal and forgiving and knows nothing of binaries or bounds. The observer sits on a vast spectrum, constantly reminding us that all of life sits on this vast spectrum, too. It has a sense of humor about it all, coaxing the performer to laugh along. It does not fear death, it does not fear life. If you listen closely, the observer can be heard cheering you on - simply because its passion lies in experience, in doing, in being.

The observer wells up with wonder as it watches you take quest after quest, fall after fall, win after win. But it has no concept of wins or losses. It just witnesses happenings as they are. With a loving gaze, the observer sits light and looming, entertained by the view.

The *performer* is of this earth, of this dimension.

The performer is limited with tools and conditions specific to this plane that allow the performer to play and interact with earth and other beings. The performer survives, pays taxes, decorates the house, chooses the proper shoes for the day, holds conversations, goes on dates, attends meetings. The performer has needs and desires, some of which do not even belong to them. The performer is just as influenced by the collective performance as it is motivated by its own solo act. The performer alternates between struggling and rejoicing in this stimulating life, a sensation often felt at great intensities.

The performer is drama, the performer is survival.

The conversation between these two forces is invisible, a potency that exists in one's own perceptive space.

Keeping these two forces acquainted is vital. The observer calms the performer, reminding the performer of its ephemerality and silly condition. The performer reminds the observer of its eternity, its freedom. The observer grows wiser as the performer takes on more acts, and the performer grows wiser as the observer witnesses more of its acts.

Flawed Translators:
Notes on the Invisible

We decipher emotions and other invisible phenomena with words, but words are not true to the form or force of the invisible, the ethereal, the energetic. Words to describe feelings are simply an attempt - an attempt at defining a non-measurable, felt sensation.

Like any translation, some gets lost - often a whole lot. You see, the invisible speaks through symbol and sensation. We are flawed translators doing our best.

How much validation do you need that the sensations you experience are real? How many times does the magic need to visit you in a form that you recognize? Just because you can't quite explain it... doesn't make it nonexistent. That sensation you have? It transcends physical language. When your tongue gets twisted and you cannot explain the thing, the moment, the feeling, the observation... that does not make it cease to exist.

What parts of you are not shared? Simply because... you don't know how to translate them to this dimension. Does it feel right when you try to translate - or does the resistance and effort hurt? Do you feel more at peace when you succumb to its nature and just listen? Interpret it telepathically, energetically as it arrives. Making no attempt to transfer it into a tangible, quantifiable medium. When you leave your body - on purpose or on accident - do you scurry back inside? When the paranormal and the transcendental visit me, in the moment, I often run back to dry land. I entertain what's possible and I am not ready. Then a part of me thinks - well, it's always there, ready when I am. Maybe some other time. The ether shares a space with death, after all. My body has a right to fear it. But isn't fear an invention of the earth? Maybe the limitations and risk found in physicality do not exist in the ether, and this reaction is senseless. In a time where so many mediums of expression are available to us, when sharing thought can be instant, when thousands of words exist to express varying existential conditions, it is easy to forget that these tools do not hold the power to decode all sensations.

Boundaries

It is good to think about your ego
and all of your DNA,
as I block someone on the internet
who is mad at me for something
that would require me to
sacrifice
a certain secrecy to defend ,
who knows nothing of it -
who kisses my surface in imagination
but claims penetration.

And I want to say

I only live for my mother and father
I only live for getting all my veggies in at breakfast
over whisked eggs
I only live for the
promise
of a gilded nothingness,
I only live for a pride
that holds two faces
and shoves me through time.
and today,
I do not hold interest
for the analysis lost
on me.
Me, who has already
left the room
in which you are desperately
measuring

Let's Get to the Root of It

if it's all about freedom and love
if it's all about feeling love
feeling freedom
if all the labor sets out to access freedom
access love
if all the effort is an effort for love
for freedom
to hold freedom, to have freedom,
to hold love, to have love,
as if it is an object or destination
something tangible
which it is not -
i vote that there is a con in place
there is a con in place that pretends
it isn't already there for you
(unseen,
available)
i vow to practice living
aware of the con
the excess
the effort
the illusion

HOME

"I only know how to do me,
so that's just what I'm going to do."

— Lana Del Rey

When People Ask Me - What Was It Like Growing Up in LA?

I want to say - it was like reaching. Reaching with long arms into any direction that would take you: the ocean, the skyline, the hills, the alleyways, the bath tub of your rich friend's Lonely mansion. It was a constant attempt at Stillness in a city of Escapism, and if not this, if you aren't careful, it is escapism on a Loop.

You know you can find that feeling you crave, and you often do: Where everything looks right until it feels right. Where the narrative is Eternal. Where every person you've ever loved sticks around, like landmarks holding the history of each identity you've taken on, of all the stories you've been a character in.

To have all of your firsts, all of your formative years, all of your lessons, in a city like this: it is like witchcraft, it is possessive. That magic plays on repeat, and a water balloon grows in the center of your chest.

Los Angeles lets you be as sprawling as the city's landscape itself and as time moves on without you, you begin to realize that you can't embrace everything in one arm-full. You can't embrace all of that energy in one big hug and you certainly can't take it all with you.

Peace comes from detaching yourself from every moment that was too good to be true but no longer belongs to you. Keeping your arms open, you find that there will always be another fleeting moment yearning to fill your chest.

Hooks

The home is messy
it all hangs from a door knob,
or a corner,
or a hook

Sometimes I think I could live
in a home of hooks
because I want to air everything out.

If all these belongings could be hung up at
eye level,
they would stay in the light
and away
from the dust,
away
from the crickets.

My belongings would always be
on the verge of an outing
on the verge of use
on the verge of importance...

The home is messy
and I am getting used to it
is it freedom
is it neglect
Don't come over
until I figure this out

Crenshaw Boulevard

my house tastes like
a rice cake on an empty stomach
or spinach and eggs fried in a pan
still greasy from yesterday

my house feels like
sitting on a washcloth
in the middle of a hot shower
my knees are up
and I am avoiding the moldy corners
like an island

my house looks like
dust that rises only to settle again
and yet another tangled power strip
bright gray against the dark laminate

my house sounds like traffic i want no part in
and the three different car crashes
that woke all five of us up at once
as we rushed to the front lawn
to witness the wreckage

When I Got My First Apartment,
I Invited My First Love to Come See It

We woke up
      to this balmy dawn
      It was the golden hour, the first golden hour
      of the two in a day,

And the stove was mine,
and the pots and pans
were mine

and the sky
was striped with
palm tree silhouettes,
their long necks.

We stepped outside
into the fallen petals
that roll in
from
      who-knows-where
They coat the floor and get
stuck to feet.

We kissed and sighed at the people
      we are now -
and I imagine you noticed that the palm trees were mine,
and the petals were mine and the stove and the pots and
the pans, and the eggs and the potatoes and the coffee
were mine -
as we kissed and sighed

during the first golden hour
of the two in a day, knowing well
that I grew up
while you were away.

I Moved Seven Homes Before My Twenty-Sixth Birthday

Moving means
coming to terms with your own illusions
Attachments
physical barriers
all that is frivolously preserved
in objects
The reality of
my nothingness

my nothingness
which is much more glamorous
when I am surrounded by density
but this
this is a true nothingness
this is a purge
this is a break up
I haven't felt this
Spacious
in a long time

Hana Highway

i live inside a dollhouse
with banana slats
like someone glued popsicle sticks together
when the cars leave the highway
and the wind isn't coming from the north
i hear the ocean and wonder
if it's actually the cars or the wind
making ocean sounds
and i ask again, and again,
if it's the cars or the wind,
a genius con,
then i decide that yes -
it really is
ocean waves
right before i fall asleep.
the light comes in at sunset,
but never at high noon,
and the washing machine
doesn't ask for any quarters,
which is a first
in my whole life
to have a washing machine
that only asks for soap

Midnight in My Home with
Two Braids and the Dryer Running

the funny thing about feeling like
the world is yours
is that it isn't like that at all.
It isn't a large force in your hands,
or a grand view from a high place.
It isn't an ownership, or an agreement.

It's heavy eyes
and a heart full of earth and heat and water,
it's an excess with no consequences.

EARTH BODY

"I am not an intellectual,
I write with my body."

— Clarice Lispector

What sensations make you want to live forever?

Help! I can't decide if dying is chill or not.

Confessions

i didn't wash the glass straw before i drank
strawberry lemonade with it,
And i accidentally used the water to clean the kettle as tea
water
And i touched my face after touching the doorknob And i
wore my shoes in the part of the house that i made a no-shoe
zone

And i worried about losing you

And i thought about aging today

to be an artist, to be an artist, to be an artist,
and to not give up

to be alive, to be alive, to be alive,
and to not give up

Sadness is Not an Alarm

it is simply a question
without any words filled in yet

and you can pretend you're on the game show
wheel of fortune
or you can dig up the whole garden
with large hands

And when the neighbor asks
what you're doing
you can tell her that you're just
hunting for treasure,
and life is so grand, so beautiful,
and that sadness
is not an alarm,
it is not a catastrophe,
it is not a family secret
it is not a tsunami warning on the local news
(so please,
just leave me alone,
and let me do all this)

Moment of Clarity No. 2:
All Forms of Maintenance, Although Pesky in the Moment, are an Action Towards Future Freedom and Bliss

I need to eat more beans and blueberries. I ordered a book on money management this morning. I once ate a banana every day for almost a year and now I find it difficult to eat one. I'd rather work to be comfortable with innate truths of existence than take part in the endless flex for perceived control. These days, I prefer rain because if I am outside, it keeps the mosquitos off of me, and if I'm inside, it's an invite to keep reading and watch the plants sway. I wonder what the summer is going to be like. I used to think abundance meant having enough to take care of everyone and now I am realizing that taking on that role is far more complex and related to childhood healing than anything. I was going to go skydiving this week but they texted me saying the plane is broken. I don't have a driver's license. If I get my license out here, it will have a rainbow on it. I can drive well, though, and once drove up the coast for seven hours without any permit. I think cars are ridiculous and take up too much space. Maybe I was rebelling against all that, mixed with some fear, and getting trapped in a cycle. I really enjoy talking to strangers, until I don't. A lot of people want way more than a moment from others. I usually just want a moment. Maybe because it's one of the few situations in which you get to be witnessed, yet undefined. When I started sharing my work publicly on the internet, I was anonymous for two years and had no interest in showing face. I have come to accept that people love seeing face, and so do I. I am extremely block happy, and I love it. Often, my driving force is an imagined enemy banking on my losses. This is why I understand Drake's music so much. I almost didn't graduate high school because my best friend and I would constantly ditch school to go swim in the only waterfall I have seen in LA, a tiny one at Temescal Canyon Park. We'd hike into the river to sunbathe and eat our school lunches naked on a rock. I'm so happy we did that.

Existence is an Infinity Mirror

Romance is a medium, sex is a medium, your body is a medium, your entire life performance is a medium. We have no choice but to express our ever-changing, unique state in every context we come into contact with. And we do this.

Are we not a planet of beings constantly coming to terms with the fact that we are both energy|ether states and matter|Earth states at varying degrees? That we live in this daunting yet wondrous body of shifting forms? That ideas can either disappear into thin air or turn into a firm object in our hands? That all the desires we act on first begin in some unknown space behind our eyes? That an unexplainable, felt connection between two humans can fuel a pleasurable union of a lifetime?

We all do a fairly similar set of human activities and yet we all do them differently. On top of that, the individual will do these activities differently throughout their lives as well. The way you eat, work, take care of yourself. The way you date, love, fuck. The way you actualize and sabotage. The *way* we do what we do is always an expression, a form of communication, thus always a medium. Nothing is a static action. We are not bots performing tasks. We are desire-driven, lusting, dripping, feeling-stricken freaks performing tasks with hot hearts and swirling heads. Decorating all of it. All of us unique in our various executions.

When everything is understood as a medium, it gets to be in its truth. Mediums are not final products. They are invitations to experiment, to tell a story the only way you know how. Mediums are full of possibilities. Mediums are ever-changing. Mediums are a desire to understand. Mediums are a collaboration between us and an outside.

Tell me that all of life is not just one grand attempt to organize all of this energy and stimulation into some sense. When senses themselves don't even ask for reason - they just offer a direct answer. Senses say - "This is how this tastes. Now goodbye." And the whole world moans.

I believe "never growing up" doesn't mean living like a child with no responsibilities - it means not becoming so jaded that you no longer feel the magnitude of your wins, the magic in the mystery, the power of playfulness. It means something as simple as your crush returning interest in you being enough to stop the world's spin and ignite a fire from scratch. It means friendship being so exquisite and giving that it makes you want to cry, makes you want to hold hands, makes you want to write long letters adorned with 3D stickers.

It's being so fucking grateful just to be outside because that's where life is. It's rewards never becoming regular, it's always having room for wishing, it's letting yourself be pleasantly surprised. It's letting things be silly, and beautiful, and possibly, somehow, entirely in your favor - because all you want in life is to experience, to see, to understand, to revel. And maybe that's the key. In having such a simple, accessible desire such as this, one is always alive.

1. the body is a channel

2. that yearns to circulate
2. that yearns to connect

3. bodies in communication
seek connection, like radio towers
hunting for a clear signal

4. when connection is achieved between
channels, it may feel like:
understanding,
freedom, harmony, trust

a sixth sense
satisfied

Moment of Clarity No. 3:
Blood Circulation as Point of Worship

To be living against all odds. To honor the gods. To be given a great gift, and to hold the wisdom to receive it. To intake beauty in its many forms. The ambiance, the meal itself. How many times we've ached and celebrated into our own personal dimensions. I am amazed that every hurt has led me here. I am amazed that every blessing has led me here. The body! Every single day! I am alive with the many worlds I can create for myself.

A life is not ruled by response or reaction. I am not a marble in a pinball machine. I am the marble, the pinball machine, the player, and the arcade itself. Zoom out and see the vibrant flow, the circulation, the spooky righteousness. Life is not as much a simulation as it is a stimulation. The way blood rushes to the sensation of heat on the skin. Circulation is my god, and the ritual of worship in service to this god is the body's steady, automated blood flow. A vessel, a channel, opening and closing to demands both real and imagined all at once. We are eternity, contained.

I Could Only Ever Be Jealous of a Ball of Gas

To compare yourself to another person, defining them as reaching a level of perfection or power beyond you, is to shove the humble truth of all human existence in the chest. None of us can cheat life, cheat death, cheat health, cheat anything. None of us experience enduring satisfaction. We are all desperately reliant, Earth-bound wanderers navigating a tangle of contradicting demands. There is never a reason to be jealous of another person. Saturn, maybe. The sun or stars, absolutely. But a person? No way.

And how united we all are, in our lack of gaseous state - our consuming, digesting bet with the tangible realm. Our flesh and weight, our unceasing maintenance. I once googled if stars eat and emit waste - what their version of that process would be, if any. Maybe it was an attempt to either humble them or increase the height of their pedestal in my mind. Or maybe it was to discover a closeness, a route in which I could become them one day. "Stars, they're just like us!" was a section in a trashy tabloid magazine I grew up perusing in the waiting room of my mother's workplace. The weekly section featured paparazzi photos of celebrities getting parking tickets or being seen at an unsavory angle in a bikini at the beach. Now I think about how humans both look up to stars in the sky and look up to stars on our screens, loving when the gap is closed by a telescope or unflattering photo.

And to answer the mystery of stars consuming, digesting, or expelling - stars consume hydrogen and emit helium. The powerful simplicity of this fact speaks of a pure energy, of an empowered internal movement, of circulation, of heat. A star is a seemingly still being, but it is far from stagnant and far from death. It churns with an energy powerful enough to endure the darkness. And isn't that what we all want?

EXERCISES IN SHAPESHIFTING

"Everything alters me,
but nothing changes me."

— Salvador Dalí

I Am Constantly Shapeshifting, Adapting, and Evolving

The first time that I integrated the mantra, "I am constantly shapeshifting, adapting, and evolving," I was attempting to define what kind of woman I was. I was dating someone new, and found myself caught between intense feelings for them and deep desires for isolation to nourish an important professional endeavor. And I kid you not, I began to wonder - am I the cold, career-driven type of woman? Or am I the nurturing, devoted type of woman?

(I know, pitiful. But I had to start somewhere.)

I recall exactly where I was when these thoughts hit - somewhere between my mattress on the floor and the toaster oven, somewhere between breakfast and the demands of the day. The way that in your early twenties, intense insights seem to call your attention with a sudden urgency and promise of relief. And this was one of those. A whole tower toppling. I realized that my entire life has been moments of introspection by way of deeply flawed binary questions like these. All day the brain asks - was this choice bad or good? Is this opinion right or wrong? Like or dislike? Happy or unhappy? We get so used to "this or that" thinking that we forget the broad, shapeshifting spectrum we all exist on. Thus, not only do these questions never get answered, they hardly even exist.

I remember feeling winded by this shift in the story, one of those mind-melting downloads. I paced around my room and attempted to recall everyone I had ever been - every identity I explored whether built for myself or for others, every personality trait embodied, every whim followed or feared. When I felt that I had discovered a steady trait in myself, I'd fish my memory for another situation in which I countered that behavior. As traits canceled each other out, it was clear that there was no overarching theme. There was no recognizable archetype fit for a sitcom character. There was no "kind of woman." Just a wide range of behaviors brought out at different times, for different purposes. What a truth. No context had ever felt more honest or freeing than the lack of any at all.

I felt that with this alone, I had solved every problem I had ever had and ever will have. Or at least, developed a destination I could travel to whenever "who am I?" grabbed at my elbows with its unwarranted urgency. I vowed to never ask myself those types of questions again. I grew skeptical of personality quizzes and modern astrology, I became concerned with all forms of mass-grouping and labeling, I became obsessed with avoiding absolutes when I spoke or wrote. I felt more present in my relationship and day-to-day, as a commitment to a simple sense of being took precedence over judging my own performance. This altered my perception of others, too, as I found myself giving them more room to breathe. I unlocked more range than any attempt at self-definition ever did. By attaching to nothing, I felt everything. In that space, I could call upon the following sentiment - I am constantly shapeshifting, adapting, and evolving.

Years later, this set of words continues to bathe me in a potent clarity as soothing as the day it first answered my foolish question.

THINGS YOU CAN PRETEND TO BE WHEN YOU FEEL UNCENTERED

Case 1: At twenty-two, following a mildly devastating heartbreak, I dragged my mattress and box spring to the center of the room and professed, "I am a lush, self-sustaining island." I then slept in the center of the room for three days. That weekend, I walked myself over to a local playhouse. A thirty-seat theater on Venice Boulevard; the space was tiny and intimate. I arrived alone in a long black dress and proceeded to watch a stubborn man fall in love with an alien. The play was incredible, surprising. I cried. Once home, I felt ready for the luxury of leaning on a wall and shoved my bed back up against it.

Case 2: Later, ready for guests and no longer isolating, I thought of myself as a castle in the desert. "Grand for itself, wise for itself," I wrote in a poem. In this new form, I was rejecting the need for outside validation, especially that of romantic partners. I imagined myself made of stone that remained cool, even at the highest noon. I imagined myself as an abundant, whimsical structure in a bare environment. Sturdy and welcoming and independent. "Grand when you arrive, grand when you leave," I added to the poem.

Case 3: In a meditation class in high school, our teacher told us to pick our place. This teacher, who did past life regression on dogs and had created a secret holistic elective under the guise of what she told her superiors would be a course on "the history of alternative medicine," said to us, "Pick a place to be in. Just sit there and listen. Make room for visits from animals, insects, spirits." I settled for a smooth, warm boulder in the sun, next to a free-flowing river, surrounded by woods. A buffalo visited me that day, my eyes closed in a classroom. When things are neutral, when things are good, when things are great, I am the boulder in the sun by the river. Or I am laying upon it.

Case 4: It's two-thousand-and-nine and I live in a moldy house off the freeway with five other people. I wish I could live alone, I wish I could break out of working retail, and every day I feel guilty for not working harder. My roommate has a cat that dominates the living room. The house cat reminds me to stretch my body and take time in the sun. The house cat makes me not feel guilty for napping too long or staring at the traffic outside. The house cat reminds me to give myself permission to relax and take it slow, and when I need to, I become her.

Some Offerings To Shift Into and Their Uses:

A LUSH, SELF-SUSTAINING ISLAND

Great vessel for...
1. Isolating with wholeness
2. Transforming feelings of loneliness into feelings of abundance
3. Finding joy in body maintenance
4. Reassessing social life
5. Committing to boundaries
6. Newfound independence
7. Manifesting financial stability

Performances:
Drag your mattress to the center of the room.
Swim out to the center of a body of water. Place a blanket in an open, grassy field and have a picnic.
Drink out of large clear glasses in direct sunlight.
Sing to your plants. Choose your friends wisely.

A CASTLE IN THE DESERT

Great vessel for...
1. Building confidence,
2. Claiming control over your energetic field,
3. Glorifying the silent, unseen labors of projects and dreams
4. Rejecting the need for attention and validation from outside forces,
5. Remaining cool and solid in moments of intensity,
6. Resilience,
7. Protection

Performances:
Go somewhere public with a journal. Ignore the gaze of others. Wear headphones on public transit. Invest in a cream, quilted coat that goes to your knees. Forget every insult. Place your hand over your belly button. Create something you don't show anybody, ever.

CLOUD IN MOVEMENT

Great vessel for...
1. Trust in yourself and the universe
2. Observing the human condition from a distance
3. Placing yourself above a situation that upsets or torments you
4. Tapping into the ether body to take a break from the the earth body
5. Making peace with ephemerality
6. Lightness
7. Shapeshifting

Performances:
Go on a bike ride on a completely flat, level road. Meditate for so long you start traveling elsewhere, or maybe you're just falling asleep. Steam your face in a small pot over the stove. Take a walk where you do nothing but listen. Witness things without words, just as entities. Visit a float tank. Forget your name.

BUSY HUMMINGBIRD

Great vessel for....
1. Embracing your work
2. Feeling capable
3. Doing necessary errands or tasks
4. Sharing yourself and your work freely without fear
5. Making peace with the pace of the internet and technology
6. Forgiving a hasty action
7. Understanding the body as a tool

Performances:
Respond to all of your emails at a busy café. Drink six different beverages in one day. Mail a postcard to every friend of yours. Put an exercise bike in front of the television and ride it until your blood circulates and your favorite show ends. Feel someone else's heartbeat on your hand. Feel invincible.

A WATERFALL

Great vessel for...
1. Dismissing any shame felt about your passionate nature
2. Embracing the sexual body
3. Channeling creative abundance
4. Making peace with changing states - as the waterfall can shift from a trickle to torrential
5. Empowered forward movement
6. Moving on from the past
7. Cleansing clarity

Performances:
Write indulgent, erotic poetry about your crush.
Do interpretive dance in open space. Drink out of a
fountain with strong water pressure. Drink an entire
glass of water in one go. Pee off of a high distance. Do
stream of consciousness writing every morning with
your tea.

A GIANT SMOOTH BOULDER IN THE SUN NEAR A BODY OF WATER

Great vessel for...
1. Noticing that your feeling of stagnation is a moment of stability
2. Pleasure in simple forms of being
3. Creating intentional moments of beauty and peace for yourself
4. Finding joy in socializing and relationships, as the boulder embraces visitors
5. Channeling balance between internal and external elements
6. Grounded observing
7. Optimal balance

Performances:
Lay in the bath and feel the water slowly rise to your
ears. Stand still in a moving crowd. Sunbathe nude in
the patch of sun that hits your bed at 2pm. Observe
your skin. Plate your dinner as if you are an artisan
chef. Go to a party and judge no one.

CERAMIC	Breaks into large, whole shards. Easy to find all pieces and clean up. Little risk to others unless they are careless. Can be put back together quite convincingly. Makes a hollow moan.
GLASS	Breaks into many sharp pieces of all sizes. High risk to all surroundings once broken. Pieces travel far and some are found weeks later or never again. Difficult to put back together, but can spend a lot of time in the ocean until it is smoothed out into beach glass. Screams loud.
PLASTIC	Breaks under pressure or won't realize it's broken it's too late and contents begin to seep out. Attempts to stay in one piece but doesn't function. When broken, mild risk to others, and if so, often surprises them. Cracks quietly and unsure, like a question.
WOOD	Breaks and splits into layers revealing the past, present, and future. When broken, a heavy energy is released that can be high risk to others if they are close enough to breathe it in or get under their skin. Holds on, only breaks for sincere reasons. Aches and echoes.

From the water's perspective, I am just another rock. I noticed this today as I stood in a pool of a rushing waterfall. The water does not feel sorry for bumping into me or annoyed that I am in its way, it does not resist nor embrace me. It just rushes, no opinion. This thought filled me with peace, embodied by a sensation of cool air down my spine and into my feet, neutralizing the heat that always exists there. I then felt the need to define this further, honor the observation with a conclusion. I stood there for a long time, fitting in with the rocks, as water moved through my legs and across my waist and caressed me with the occasional twig.

Vinicius joined me and we stood there like rocks together. I said, "If we stay here long enough, we will become eroded," which was great to imagine, but then I started thinking of my skin being different material than a rock and realized this statement is probably untrue. In fact, I just googled it, and being submerged in water for days *would* cause you to erode, but in a far less graceful way. It says open sores would form. The point is - I have not yet found any poetry in eroding, but marveling at the relationship between the rushing water and my stationary form opened another portal in which to witness interaction.

There are many situations in which there is flowing water and a rock present - stimulation and a body, a body and another body, a call to reaction or response, a space between two interacting points. Even within the self. And we fill that space with all kinds of stories and judgements, many of which shift rapidly as our feelings do, unreliable in their range of definition. To pause and assume the position of the water or the rock is to align with the less dramatic truth of what is. It is to diminish the urge to battle and react, and instead revel in pure sentience. It is to close the gap between two points and simply let them be.

1. Step off of the hamster wheel.
1. Step off of the carousel.
2. Take it all in at once.
3. Do this frequently.

1. Step off of the hamster wheel.
1. Step off of the carousel.
2. Take it all in at once.
3. Do this frequently.

1. Step off of the hamster wheel.
1. Step off of the carousel.
2. Take it all in at once.
3. Do this frequently.

(I have no choice
but to enjoy
the *infinity mirror*.
I appreciate
that at least
the aesthetic of it all
changes
as the truth plays
on a loop.)

This book is dedicated to every person who encouraged me to get my words off their social media feeds and into their bookshelves and beds instead. To my Tumblr blog I began in the ninth grade and never stopped writing into - the "create a text post" box becoming my very first studio space as long as I got my turn on the family computer. To the many mugs of green tea. To my parents who made sure we all ate dinner together every night, who taught me that joy is simple and life is an adventure. To my mother's consistent laughter and my father's passion for spirituality. And most of all, this book is dedicated to the invisible - all of its sensations and mysteries that make life so dimensional.